Introduction

Current events can cause overwhelming fear and terror. There is chaos and unrest all around. The future seems so dark, unsettled and cloudy.

Did you know that even in this, you can experience clarity, direction, meaning, purpose, comfort, joy and hope for your life? The good news is found in Jesus Christ, he is the answer! This is why he is called the Light of the World.

God offers an extraordinary and priceless gift to you, that no money can buy, no one can steal and that continually brings peace, security and eternal hope.

Praying that this message will encourage you and impact your life in a significant and meaningful way.

Daily Topics

Day 1- God's Greatness and Holiness

Day 2- Created by God

Day 3- The Devastation of Sin

Day 4- The Sacrifice of Love Jesus Made for You

Day 5- God's Gift of Salvation

Day 6- Understanding God's Grace and Forgiveness

Day 7- The Hope of Heaven

Day 8- The Joy in Christ's Return

Day 9- Your Heritage in Christ

Day 10- God is Your Refuge

Day 11- God is With You

Day 12- God has a Purpose for Your Life

Day 13- The Peace of Christ

Day 1

God's Greatness and Holiness

Great:

CHIEF; OF VAST POWER AND EXCELLENCE; SUPREME; ILLUSTRIOUS; AS THE GREAT GOD; THE GREAT CREATOR

The Bible says...

For since the creation of the world His invisible attributes, His eternal power and divine nature, have been clearly seen, being understood through what has been made, so that they are without excuse.

ROMANS 1:20

We can learn about God and know that he is real by looking around at all he has made. Think about stars, your favorite animal or a beautiful place in nature. Aren't these wonderful? They all tell of God's greatness. There are many complex mysteries about God's creations that scientists have yet to understand.

Your, O Lord, is the greatness and the power and the glory and the victory and the majesty, indeed everything that is in heavens and the Earth, Yours is the dominion, O Lord, and You exalt Yourself as head over all.

1 CHRONICLES 29:11

God has always existed, even before he created the world. He is the author of time, the all powerful God who is to be revered and honored. He is in charge of all creation.

"HOLY, HOLY, HOLY is THE LORD GOD, THE ALMIGHTY, WHO WAS AND WHO IS AND WHO IS TO COME."
REVELATION 4:8

God resides in Heaven surrounded by angels and heavenly beings. He is the ruler of the entire universe. He is perfect and pure.

Bless the LORD, O my soul! O LORD my God, You are very great; You are clothed with splendor and majesty…
PSALM 104:1

God is glorious and full of splendor and majesty. He deserves honor and praise.

Praying for you…

~That you would understand how excellent and great God is, he rules the universe with power and might. He set the world in motion and all of creation tells of who he is and his everlasting greatness.

~That you will get a glimpse of the mighty and extraordinary power of God.

Great is the Lord, His Power is Great

Great is the Lord, His power is great, my tongue His mighty acts relate:
Adore and fear the sovereign Lord, who rules all nature by His word.

He speaks—the gathering clouds obey; thick darkness veils the face of day;
Swift lightnings burst the pitchy cloud, and awful thunders roar aloud.

Roused at His call the winds awake, and from their wings destruction shake;
With groans the bending woods resound, and cast their honors to the ground.

On mounting waves the sailors rise, they seem to touch the very skies;
Instant they plunge with dreadful hiss, o'erwhelmed and lost in the abyss.

Well may poor mortals fear and quake, his voice makes hills and mountains shake:
Far o'er the land the billows dash, and cities fall with hideous crash.

He speaks—the winds their fury cease, the raging waves are hushed to peace,
   Nature her calmest look puts on, well pleased the sudden night is gone.

Great is the Lord, His power is great, my tongue His mighty acts relate:
   Adore and fear the sovereign Lord, who rules all nature by His word.

JOHN NEEDHAM, 1768

Day 2

You are Created by God

Create:

TO BEGET, TO GENERATE, TO BRING FORTH

The Bible says...

In the beginning God created the heavens and the earth.

Genesis 1:1

In the beginning, God started this world and created every living thing. He made the heavens and the earth. This same God created you.

I will give thanks to You, for I am fearfully and wonderfully made; wonderful are Your works, and my soul knows it very well.

Psalm 139:14

Everyone created by God is fearfully and wonderfully made and important to him.

For You formed my inward parts; you wove me in my mother's womb.

Psalm 139:13

God was making and creating you before you were even born! He saw you as he formed you.

The Spirit of God has made me, and the breath of the Almighty gives me life.

Job 33:4

God is the one who gives you life and breath. He has a plan for you.

...just as He chose us in Him before the foundation of the world, that we would be holy and blameless before Him.

EPHESIANS 1:4

God is so powerful and all knowing, before the creation of the world he knew you. He already knew about your existence before you actually existed.

Praying for you...

~Thanking God that he made you. He made the sky, the billions of stars, the moon and all of creation, and he created you.

~That you will know how much God cares for you.

~That you would understand your purpose and worth.

~That you would have a deep sense of value and belonging because God loves you.

All Things Bright and Beautiful...

All things bright and beautiful, all creatures great and small,
All things wise and wonderful, the Lord God made them all.

Each little flow'r that opens, each little bird that sings,
He made their glowing colors, he made their tiny wings.

The purple-headed mountain, the river running by,
The sunset, and the morning that brightens up the sky.

The cold wind in the winter, the pleasant summer sun,
The ripe fruits in the garden, he made them, ev'ry one.

The tall trees in the greenwood, the meadows where we play,
The flowers by the water we gather ev'ry day.

He gave us eyes to see them, and lips that we might tell
How great is God Almighty, who has made all things well.

CECIL FRANCES ALEXANDER, 1848

Day 3

The Devastation of Sin

Sin:

TO DEPART VOLUNTARILY FROM THE PATH OF DUTY PRESCRIBED BY GOD TO MAN; TO VIOLATE THE DIVINE LAW IN ANY PARTICULAR, BY ACTUAL TRANSGRESSION OR BY THE NEGLECT OR NON-OBSERVANCE OF ITS INJUNCTIONS…

The Bible says...

The Lord God gave the man [Adam] this order: You are free to eat from any of the trees of the garden except the tree of knowledge of good and evil. From that tree you shall not eat; when you eat from it you shall die.
GENESIS 2:16

He [the Devil as a snake] asked the woman [Eve], "Did God really say, 'You shall not eat from any of the trees in the garden'?"..."You certainly will not die!"
GENESIS 3:4

Satan, also known as the devil, was one of God's angels. He disobeyed God and now he is the enemy of God, trying to deceive and lie to people. Satan tempted the first man and woman, Adam and Eve, and they sinned by choosing to disobey God. As a result of this, sin entered the human heart and people and God are now separated because of sin.

Now the deeds of the flesh are evident, which are: immorality, impurity, sensuality, idolatry, sorcery, enmities, strife, jealousy, outbursts of anger, disputes, dissensions, factions, envying, drunkenness, carousing, and things like these...
GALATIANS 5:19-21

Sin is the opposite of what God wants. For example, God wants morality, kindness, purity, peace, soberness and love. Sin goes against all things good.

...for all have sinned and fall short of the glory of God...
ROMANS 3:23

Sins are the wrong things that we do. God is a pure and flawless being who can not tolerate sin. When we sin it hurts God deeply. Every person has sinned and gone against God's perfect will.

...the blazing furnace, where there will be weeping and gnashing of teeth.
MATTHEW 13:42

God lives in Heaven, a beautiful, joyful and amazing place. Because of sin, we are destined for an eternity separated from God. That miserable place is called hell. There is nothing good or cheerful in hell. The only thing that happens there is evil and terrible suffering with a complete absence from God's presence, goodness and glory.

Praying for you, that you...

~Will see how sin, and the evil of the human heart, separates us from a holy and loving God.

~Can understand more about what sin is, how it hurts you and how it brings a devastating eternity apart from God.

~Will have a clear picture of the danger and horror of sin and know that a world with sin is not what God intended or wanted when he made you and his creation.

Sin Can Never Enter There

Heaven is a holy place, filled with glory and with grace-
Sin can never enter there;
All within its gates are pure, from defilement kept secure-
Sin can never enter there.

Sin can never enter there, Sin can never enter there;
So if at the judgment bar sinful spots your soul shall mar,
You can never enter there.

If you hope to dwell at last, when your life on earth is past, in that home so bright and fair, you must here be cleansed from sin,
Have the life of Christ within- sin can never enter there.

You may live in sin below, Heaven's grace refuse to know,
But you cannot enter there; it will stop you at the door,
Bar you out forevermore- sin can never enter there.

If you cling to sin till death, when you draw your latest breath,
> You will sink in dark despair to the regions of the lost,
> Thus to prove at awful cost, sin can never enter there.

>> Charles W. Naylor, 1899

Farewell to Sin.

I will part with thee, old master; this is my firm resolve;
And I'll boldly state my reason, why we must now dissolve.

The wages of sin is death, the wages of sin is death,
The wages of sin is death, and woe, and bitter remorse; I've found it so;
Bitter, bitter, bitter remorse and woe.

I have served thee [sin] long and faithful, confessed you were my lord;
All your way was dark and painful, and what is my reward?

I have given time and talents, my health and honor, too,
And exposed my soul to torments, and what did you bestow?

You have flattered me, and promised much pleasure in your reign;
I have sowed and reaped your harvest, now what my wretched gain?

While beneath your doleful bondage, how oft your father came,
Saying, "There is here no passage out from your dark domain."

But the blood of my Redeemer has saved me through and through,
So, in Jesus' name, forever I bid all sin adieu.

DANIEL S. WARNER, 1893

Day 4

The Sacrifice of Love Jesus Made for You

Sacrifice:

To destroy, surrender or suffer to be lost for the sake of obtaining something

The Bible says...

You know that He appeared in order to take away sins; and in Him there is no sin.

1 JOHN 3:5

Jesus was perfect. He willingly came from Heaven to Earth as God's son. He lived as a man and never committed a single sin.

For God so loved the world, that He gave His only begotten Son, that whoever believes in Him shall not perish, but have eternal life.

JOHN 3:16

The punishment for sin is death and an eternity in hell away from God. God put all the punishment of sin, that should have been ours, on his precious and perfect son Jesus, whom he loved.

He [God] made Him [Jesus] who knew no sin to be sin on our behalf, so that we might become the righteousness of God in Him.

1 CORINTHIANS 5:21

God loves you so much that he sent Jesus, as a willing and perfect gift, to sacrifice his life for you.

But He was pierced through for our transgressions, He was crushed for our iniquities; The chastening for our well-being fell upon Him, and by His scourging we are healed.

Isaiah 53:5

All the punishment that we deserve was placed on Jesus. He paid the price that should have been ours. Because of this, there is a wonderful opportunity to have a relationship with God and to be close to God, just like God intended when he made the world.

Praying for you, that you know...

~How much Jesus loves you and how he willingly died on the cross for your sins. He took your punishment upon himself.

~How deeply God loves you and that there is nothing you can do that will change the depth of God's love for you.

Crucified for Me

Prince of glory condescended, He has favored me;
On the cross He meekly suffered my poor soul to free;
He has cleansed my inner being, changed my life of wrong;
How His touch of healing virtue fills my heart with song!

He was crucified for me, He was crucified for me, He was crucified for me,
On the cross of Calvary.

Oh, what consolation offered in His righteousness,
From the highest realm of glory coming down to this!
Here in gloomy maze He found me, languishing to die,
But the light from heaven streaming cleared my mortal sky.

When the pall of night was lifted hope began to start;
When the clouds so thick were rifted, light shone in my heart,
When the shock from Calv'ry's mountain shook my sinful soul,
Then the stream from that blest fountain over me did roll.

See the Sov'reign of creation, King of earth and skies,
All for sinful man's salvation thus He dies, He dies;
Yet He lives, a mighty Monarch, reigns o'er every foe,
Causing mortal man to triumph over sin below.

Barney E. Warren, 1900

Day 5

The Gift of Salvation

Gift:

A PRESENT; ANY THING GIVEN OR BESTOWED; ANY THING, THE PROPERTY OF WHICH IS VOLUNTARILY TRANSFERRED BY ONE PERSON TO ANOTHER WITHOUT COMPENSATION

The Bible says...

He was buried, and...He was raised on the third day...
1 CORINTHIANS 15:4

Jesus died, but the wonderful news is that God is more powerful than death. Jesus conquered death and came back to life. He rose up to Heaven and now is seated next to God.

...that if you confess with your mouth Jesus as Lord, and believe in your heart that God raised Him from the dead, you will be saved...
ROMANS 10:9

If you choose to say that Jesus is Lord and put him in charge of your life, if you believe in your heart that Jesus died for your sins and rose up from the dead, then all your sins will be forgiven.

"Come now, and let us reason together," says the LORD, "Though your sins are as scarlet, they will be as white as snow; though they are red like crimson, they will be like wool..."
ISAIAH 1:18

God offers a free gift to you, which is complete forgiveness. If you accept Jesus and ask him to take charge of your life, your sins will be forgiven. This fixes the broken relationship between you and God. You can now be close to God and God views you as pure, holy and sinless because of what Jesus did for you.

"In the same way, I tell you, there is joy in the presence of the angels of God over one sinner who repents."

Luke 15:10

When we repent of our sins to God, acknowledge our wrongs and turn to Jesus, the angels in Heaven have great joy. They celebrate because the best decision was made. There is now life instead of death inside the person who asks God for help and forgiveness.

Praying for you that...

~You will know that Jesus died for you on the cross.

~God will work in your heart and life so that you can come to a decision to commit your life to him.

~This free gift of salvation and a forever home in Heaven will be yours.

It was Jesus Who Set Me Free

When I was treading the pathway of wrong,
When I was bound by the fetters so strong,
When I had lost all my sunshine and song, it was Jesus who set me free.

It was Jesus who set me free,
It was Jesus who set me free;
Now every chain has been broken in twain, it was Jesus who set me free.

When for my soul there was no one to care,
When condemnation seemed mine everywhere,
When I was bound by the chains of despair, it was Jesus who set me free.

When on my pathway no light seemed to shine, when I was dreading the judgment divine,
When evil powers seemed all to combine, it was Jesus who set me free.

When I am singing His glory and praise, marvelous, wonderful, infinite grace,
That He should suffer and die in my place- it was Jesus who set me free.

HALDOR LILLENAS, 1915

Day 6

God's Grace and Forgiveness

Grace:

THE FREE UNMERITED LOVE AND FAVOR OF GOD, THE SPRING AND SOURCE OF ALL THE BENEFITS MEN RECEIVE FROM HIM

The Bible says...

For as high as the heavens are above the earth, so great is His lovingkindness toward those who fear Him. As far as the east is from the west, so far has He removed our transgressions from us.

PSALM 103:11-12

Because of what Jesus did on the cross and because God loves us so much, there is complete forgiveness for every sin. God removes our sins. They are gone and no more.

He straightened up, and said to them, "He who is without sin among you, let him be the first to throw a stone at her." Again He stooped down and wrote on the ground. When they heard it, they began to go out one by one, beginning with the older ones, and He was left alone, and the woman, where she was, in the center of the court. Straightening up, Jesus said to her, "Woman, where are they? Did no one condemn you?" She said, "No one, Lord." And Jesus said, "I do not condemn you, either. Go. From now on sin no more.

JOHN 8:7-11

This is a perfect example of what Jesus does. He does not condemn us for our sins if we ask him to forgive us. He makes us clean and then we can have a new start to make better choices with his help.

But if it is by grace, it is no longer on the basis of works, otherwise grace is no longer grace.

ROMANS 11:6

God's grace and mercy can not be earned. You can not work to earn salvation, God's love or his favor. All of this has already been given to you by God out of his grace and mercy if you accept Jesus.

Praying for you that...

~You can learn more about who Jesus is and understand how he died for all sins.
~ You will learn more about God's incredible grace and forgiveness.
~You will experience God's grace and forgiveness in a deep and personal way.
~You will know God's unconditional love for you.

Wonderful Grace of Jesus.

Wonderful grace of Jesus, greater than all my sin;
How shall my tongue describe it, where shall its praise begin?
Taking away my burden, setting my spirit free;
For the wonderful grace of Jesus reaches me.

Wonderful the matchless grace of Jesus, deeper than the mighty rolling sea;
Higher than the mountain, sparkling like a fountain,
All-sufficient grace for even me!

Broader than the scope of my transgressions, greater far than all my sin and
Shame; oh, magnify the precious Name of Jesus, Praise His Name!
Wonderful grace of Jesus, reaching to all the lost,
By it I have been pardoned, saved to the uttermost;
Chains have been torn asunder, giving me liberty;
For the wonderful grace of Jesus reaches me.

Wonderful grace of Jesus, reaching the most defiled,
By its transforming power, making him God's dear child,
Purchasing peace and Heaven for all eternity-
And the wonderful grace of Jesus reaches me.

Haldor Lillenas, 1918

Come While He is Calling

If, dear sinner, you are longing all those sinful chains to break,
And relieve your soul from anguish, which no human form can take,
Then decide this very moment, that from bondage you'll be free;
Heed, oh, heed His wooing Spirit, come and He will pardon thee.

Then, oh, come while He is calling, lay your burden at His feet;
He will take away all anguish, if His promise you will meet.

Oh, dear sinner, do not tarry, when your soul in peril lies,
Though your sins be great like mountains, tow'ring upward to the skies;
For, from every one He'll free you, and a refuge He will be;
He's the blessed Rock of Ages that was cleft for you and me.

Turn, dear sinner, from the evils that have laden down your heart,
And have made your home unhappy- tis the demon's fiery dart;
Turn, oh, turn to Christ, our Savior, and for Him yield fruits of love,
Which will prove to all a blessing, and will crown your soul above.

NOAH H. BYRUM, 1897

How can someone become a Christian?

1) Understand that you have sinned and fallen short of God's glory.

...for all have sinned and fall short of the glory of God...Romans 3:23

2) Know that the wages of sin is an eternity of death.

For the wages of sin is death...Romans 6:23a

3) Understand that God gives you a free gift which is eternal life in Christ Jesus our Lord.

...but the free gift of God is eternal life in Christ Jesus our Lord...Romans 6:23b

4) Declare that Jesus is Lord and believe in your heart that God raised Him from the dead.

That if you confess with your mouth Jesus as Lord, and believe in your heart that God raised Him from the dead, you will be saved...Romans 10:9

A salvation prayer...

Dear Jesus, I am sorry for my sins. Thank you for taking my sins away by dying on the cross. I believe you were buried and then rose from the dead. I believe you returned to Heaven, and from there, you rule and reign. Please come into my life. I give you my life and surrender myself to you. Thank you that you love me and that I am now your child!

If you made the decision to follow Jesus, write down the date and celebrate!

Day 7

The Hope of Heaven

Hope:

CONFIDENCE IN A FUTURE EVENT; THE HIGHEST DEGREE OF WELL FOUNDED EXPECTATION OF GOOD; AS A HOPE FOUNDED ON GOD'S GRACIOUS PROMISES; A SCRIPTURAL SENSE

The Bible says...

...and He will wipe away every tear from their eyes; and there will no longer be any death; there will no longer be any mourning, or crying, or pain; the first things have passed away." And He [God] who sits on the throne said, "Behold, I am making all things new." And He said, "Write, for these words are faithful and true."

REVELATION 21: 4-5

The words of the LORD are pure words; as silver tried in a furnace on the earth, refined seven times.

PSALM 12:6

For those who make the decision to follow Jesus, there are some promises from God. God promises once in Heaven, he will wipe all tears from their eyes, there will be no more death, pain, sickness or suffering. When God says this, it is true because his words are pure and honest.

Death is swallowed up in victory. O death, where is your victory? O death, where is your sting?

1 CORINTHIANS 15:54-55

Death is all around us in this sin filled world. However, Jesus conquered and defeated death through his resurrection. After death, if we believe in Jesus, we immediately are welcomed into Heaven. God also promises that each of us will get a new eternal body, superior to this earthly body.

In My Father's house are many dwelling places; if it were not so, I would have told you; for I go to prepare a place for you. If I go and prepare a place for you, I will come again and receive you to Myself, that where I am, there you may be also.

JOHN 14:2-3

Heaven is a place where those who believe in Jesus will live. If you accept and believe the good news about what Jesus did, he will prepare a wonderful and special place in Heaven just for you. It will be perfect and stunning.

Praying for you that...

~You will learn more about the truth of Heaven. It is more glorious than we can even imagine. It will be so spectacular, exciting and remarkable. There is pure joy and peace in Heaven, nothing painful, scary or evil. Death will be gone.

~You will know if you believe in Jesus, you will live forever in Heaven.

Saint's Reward

Life on earth is but a vapor, soon we'll lay these bodies down;
But if we continue faithful, we shall wear the victor's crown-
Brighter than the stars of heaven, brighter than the dazzling sun,
We shall shine among the ransomed, when our work on earth is done.

We shall not abide forever in this gloomy vale of tears,
For our life shall, at the longest, only last a few short years;
Then we'll fly away to glory, at our Father's own right hand,
Help to sing redemption's story with the blood-washed angel band.

I would not give up my title to that future world of bliss
For the shining gold and silver of a thousand worlds like this;
I would rather bear affliction, be a hated pilgrim here,
Miss the diadems terrestrial, and obtain a crown up there.

Let us then be up and doing, we have but a few more days,
Priceless souls of men to rescue from their dark and sinful ways;
Courage, brother, work and suffer, till this fleeting life is past;
God will recompense our labors with a great reward at last.

WILLIAM G. SCHELL, 1900

Day 8

The Joy in Christ's Return

Return:

THE ACT OF COMING OR GOING BACK TO THE SAME PLACE

The Bible says...

But we do not want you to be uninformed, brethren, about those who are asleep, so that you will not grieve as do the rest who have no hope. For if we believe that Jesus died and rose again, even so God will bring with Him those who have fallen asleep in Jesus. For this we say to you by the word of the Lord, that we who are alive and remain until the coming of the Lord, will not precede those who have fallen asleep. For the Lord Himself will descend from Heaven with a shout, with the voice of the archangel and with the trumpet of God, and the dead in Christ will rise first. Then we who are alive and remain will be caught up together with them in the clouds to meet the Lord in the air, and so we shall always be with the Lord. Therefore comfort one another with these words.

1 THESSALONIANS 4:13-18

Just as Jesus went back up to Heaven after he rose from the grave, he is going to come back to Earth. He is going to retrieve all those who belong to him. This is comforting, because this life is just temporary and short compared to our eternal life, with Jesus, in Heaven.

For the grace of God has appeared, bringing salvation to all men, instructing us to deny ungodliness and worldly desires and to live sensibly, righteously and godly in the present age, looking for the blessed hope and the appearing of the glory of our great God and Savior, Christ Jesus, who gave Himself for us to redeem us from every lawless deed, and to purify for Himself a people for His own possession, zealous for good deeds.
TITUS 2:11-14

Living for Jesus and honoring him with your life is the best way to prepare for his approaching return.

Behold, I tell you a mystery; we will not all sleep, but we will all be changed, in a moment, in the twinkling of an eye, at the last trumpet; for the trumpet will sound, and the dead will be raised imperishable, and we will be changed. For this perishable must put on the imperishable, and this mortal must put on immortality.
I CORINTHIANS 15:51-53

When Jesus returns, our bodies will change. We will have wonderful bodies with no illnesses or problems. We will have bodies that last forever.

But of that day and hour no one knows...For this reason you also must be ready; for the Son of Man is coming at an hour when you do not think He will.

Matthew 24:36 and 44

No one knows when Jesus will return. It is important to make the critical decision to follow him now, before it is too late.

Praying for you that...

~You will know that Jesus is real and that he is coming back one day. He may come back within our lifetime.

~You will come to know Jesus and experience the joy and gladness that will fill the hearts of those who love him when he returns on that long awaited, very exciting and glorious day.

We Know Not the Hour

We know not the hour of the Master's appearing, yet signs all foretell that the moment is nearing. When He shall return-'tis a promise most cheering- but we know not the hour.

He will come, let us watch and be ready; He will come, hallelujah! Hallelujah! He will come in the clouds of His Father's bright glory- but we know not the hour.

There's light for the wise who are seeking salvation, there's truth in the Book of divine revelation- each prophecy points to the great consummation- but we know not the hour.

We'll watch and we'll pray, with our lamps trimmed and burning, we'll work and we'll wait till the Master's returning, we'll sing and rejoice, every omen discerning- but we know not the hour.

FRANKLIN E. BELDEN, 1886

Day 9

Your Heritage in Christ

Heritage:

THE SAINTS OR PEOPLE OF GOD ARE CALLED HIS HERITAGE AS BEING CLAIMED BY HIM, AND THE OBJECTS OF HIS SPECIAL CARE

The Bible says...

But you are a chosen people, a royal priesthood, a holy nation, a people for God's own possession, so that you may proclaim the excellencies of Him who has called you out of darkness into His marvelous light; for you once were not a people, but now you are the people of God; you had not received mercy, but now you have received mercy.

1 PETER 2:9

If you accept Jesus, you become royal and set apart. You are his possession, rescued and called away from sin and darkness. You are now safe in God's merciful arms.

"And I will be a father to you, and you shall be sons and daughters to Me," says the Lord Almighty.

2 CORINTHIANS 6:18

If you commit your life to Jesus, you become God's precious child. You belong to him and now have the status as the child of the Almighty God! He gave his son Jesus so that you could be his.

If you then, being evil, know how to give good gifts to your children, how much more will your Father who is in Heaven give what is good to those who ask Him!
MATTHEW 7:11

Earthly fathers and mothers can fail miserably but God is your perfect and good Father in Heaven. He will watch over you, take care of you and give you his pure and unconditional love.

See how great a love the Father has bestowed on us, that we would be called children of God; and such we are. For this reason the world does not know us, because it did not know Him.
1 JOHN 3:1

God's love is so great for you that he was willing to die. He longs to call you his child and make you his own.

Praying for you...

~*That you will know God's deep love and that he wants you to be his child.*
~*That you realize a rich and beautiful inheritance can be yours in Christ, and that you are royalty in God's eyes, if you have put your trust in Christ.*

Because He Loves Me...

When the storm winds rage, and the rain falls fast, and the clouds hang low
above, I shall be secure till the storm is past, for I trust my Savior's love.
And He knows the way, and He holds my hand, and He will not let it go;
He will lead me home to that better land, just because He loves me so.

It was not that I was so good or great, for my heart was vile with sin;
I had turned my back on the narrow gate, neither care nor lived for Him,
But I pleased myself, and I chose my way, for His grace I did not know;
But He sought me still through the night and day, just because He loved me so.

If He loved me so when I grieved Him sore that He sought me tenderly,
Till He won my heart, and my sins He bore, so that I His child might be,
Will He love me less since I love Him, too, so my heart with fervor glows?
And I haste each day all His will to do that my willing spirit knows.

I will trust His love, for it e'er will last, it is rich and warm and free;
Through the years of life it will hold me fast, and my help and comfort be;
To my waiting heart all its treasures rare as a sparkling stream shall flow;
In the joy of God I shall ever share, just because He loves me so.

> Charles W. Naylor, 1917

Day 10

God is Your Refuge

Refuge:

THAT WHICH SHELTERS OR PROTECTS FROM DANGER, DISTRESS OR CALAMITY; A STRONG HOLD WHICH PROTECTS BY ITS STRENGTH, OR A SANCTUARY WHICH SECURES SAFETY BY ITS SACREDNESS; ANY PLACE INACCESSIBLE TO AN ENEMY.

The Bible says...

God is our refuge and strength, a very present help in trouble. Therefore we will not fear, though the earth should change and though the mountains slip into the heart of the sea; Though its waters roar and foam, though the mountains quake at its swelling pride.

PSALM 46:1-3

God is right there with you in the midst of trouble. He is holding your hand and standing by you. He can be your source of strength when you feel like you have nothing left. He can be the one you turn to when the world around you is crashing down in chaos. Nothing is too great for him. For those who belong to Jesus, no trouble can separate them from the love and grace of God, or steal from them the promise of a secure eternity in heaven.

The Lord is my rock and my fortress and my deliver, My God, my rock, in whom I take refuge; my shield and the horn of my salvation, my stronghold.

PSALM 18:2

Sometimes you may feel like there is no one to run to. You may feel trapped as if the ground is falling from under your feet. God can hold you up and deliver you from evil.

The name of the Lord is a strong tower; the righteous run into it and are safe.
PROVERBS 18:10

When you feel scared and alone, cry out to Jesus because he will help you. Call to him and you will feel his presence and protection.

The Lord also will be a stronghold for the oppressed, a stronghold in times of trouble, and those who know Your name will put their trust in You, for You, O Lord, have not forsaken those who seek You.
PSALM 9:9-10

When you feel oppressed and when you are struggling, that is when God shows up. If you know him and put your trust in him, he will work in some miraculous and unexpected ways. God will not forsake those who belong to him.

Praying for you that...

~You can know and turn to the Lord when you need help.
~You will understand that God is safe, good and reliable and he is right by your side, ready to be you source of strength, if you ask him.
~You will know that your eternity is completely secure if you belong to Jesus.

Within the Rock

I have a sure and safe retreat to which I always flee,
from every storm of life I meet- tis Christ the Rock for me.

Within the Rock I safely hide, a glorious place for me;
There's naught more sure that can abide through time or eternity.

Though tempests rage and wild winds blow, whom can I trust but Thee?
I feel secure from every foe in Christ, the Rock for me.

Come stormy wind and rolling sea, come fire and tempest shock,
I'm in that cleft once made for me in Christ the solid Rock.

Barney E. Warren, 1900

Day 11

God is With You

With:

IN COMPANY

The Bible says...

But the Lord is faithful, and He will strengthen and protect you from the evil one.

2 THESSALONIANS 3:3

When we belong to Jesus, we can trust that God will give us strength in any situation. He will be our protector and defender from Satan. He is actively guarding and shielding those who belong to him.

The Lord is my shepherd, I shall not want. He makes me lie down in green pastures; He leads me beside quiet waters. He restores my soul; He guides me in the paths of righteousness for His name's sake. Even though I walk through the valley of the shadow of death, I fear no evil, for You are with me; your rod and Your staff, they comfort me. You prepare a table before me in the presence of my enemies; You have anointed my head with oil; my cup overflows. Surely goodness and lovingkindness will follow me all the days of my life, and I will dwell in the house of the Lord forever.

PSALM 23:1-6

Just as a shepherd watches over and cares for sheep, God is watching over you. He brings good things into your life. He is there in scary times, walking right beside you. He is there when you are surrounded by enemies. He promises that those who love him will spend eternity in Heaven with him.

You have enclosed me behind and before, and laid Your hand upon me.
PSALM 139:5

God goes ahead of you and behind you. He has been there in the hardest of times and already knows what your future holds. He is with you now. His hand is upon you. He is guiding you and leading you. He has good plans for you. His presence is surrounding you.

I will ask the Father, and He will give you another Helper, that He may be with you forever;
JOHN 14:16

Jesus promises the Holy Spirit, who is our Helper and advocate. He is there to comfort and give discretion. He is with those who believe.

Praying for you that you will...

~Experience the reality of God's presence in your life.
~Know God is right beside you this very day. He sees your situation and will be with you through every trial. He can be your strength, help, protector and guide if you call out to him.

My Father Watches Over Me...

I trust in God wherever I may be, upon the land, or on the rolling sea,
For come what may, from day to day, my heav'nly Father watches over me.

I trust in God, I know He cares for me; on mountain bleak or on the stormy sea;
Though billows roll, He keeps my soul; my heav'nly Father watches over me.

He makes the rose an object of His care, He guides the eagle through the pathless air, and surely He remembers me; my heav'nly Father watches over me.

I trust in God, for, in the lion's den, on battlefield, or in the prison pen,
Through praise or blame, through flood or flame, my heav'nly Father watches over me.

The valley may be dark, the shadows deep, but, oh, the Shepherd guards His lonely sheep; and through the gloom He'll lead me home, My heav'nly Father watches over me.

WILLIAM C. MARTIN, 1910

Day 12

God Has a Purpose for Your Life

Purpose:

TO INTEND; TO DESIGN; TO RESOLVE; TO DETERMINE ON SOME END OR OBJECT TO BE ACCOMPLISHED

The Bible says...

Your [God's] eyes have seen my unformed substance; and in Your book were all written the days that were ordained for me, when as yet there was not one of them. How precious also are Your thoughts to me, O God! How vast is the sum of them! If I should count them, they would outnumber the sand...
PSALM 139:16-18

God knew you before you were born. He knew everything about you, how long you will live and what you will become. He thinks about you and cares for you so much, that all his thoughts for you outnumber the grains of sand!

And we know that God causes all things to work together for good to those who love God, to those who are called according to His purpose.
ROMANS 8:28

For the person who has committed their life to Jesus, God will work in their life. He has a purpose and a plan. He will take every situation, every difficult trial, and turn these around into something that will work for your good.

To comfort all who mourn, to grant those who mourn in Zion, giving them a garland instead of ashes, the oil of gladness instead of mourning, the mantle of praise instead of a spirit of fainting. So they will be called oaks of righteousness, the planting of the Lord, that He may be glorified.

ISAIAH 61:1-3

God can take the brokenness in your life, the lost hope, the hurt and the ashes of pain and disappointment and turn these into something beautiful. He can work in your life and turn your sorrow into joy. He can firmly establish you as a righteous strong pillar of strength. God is glorious and is able to do the impossible if you invite him to work in your life.

Praying for you that...

~You will know God has good plans for you. He knew you since before you were born. God knows the hurt and pain you have experienced.

~God will work in your life and heart to fulfill his purposes for you.

~You would know that in any situation you are facing right now, God is there to help. He will show you what to do and guide you toward your purpose in life if you call to him.

God's Way is Best

God's way is best; if human wisdom a fairer way may seem to show,
It's only that our earth-dimmed vision the truth can never clearly know.

God's way is best, I will not murmur, although the end I may not see;
Where'er He leads I'll meekly follow, God's way is best, is best for me.

Had I the choosing of my pathway, in blindness I should go astray,
And wander far away in darkness, nor reach that land of endless day.

He leadeth true; I will not question, though through the valley I shall go;
Though I should pass through clouds of trial, and drink the cup of human woe.

God's way is best; heart, cease thy struggling to see and know and understand;
Forsake thy fears and doubts, but trusting, submit thyself into His hand.

Thy way is best, so lead me onward, my all I give to Thy control;
Thy loving hand will truly guide me, and safe to glory bring my soul.

CHARLES W. NAYLOR, 1904

Day 13

The Peace of Christ

Peace:

FREEDOM FROM AGITATION OR DISTURBANCE...AS FROM FEAR, TERROR, ANGER, ANXIETY OR THE LIKE; QUIETNESS OF MIND; TRANQUILITY; CALMNESS; QUIET OF CONSCIENCE

The Bible says...

Be anxious for nothing, but in everything by prayer and supplication with thanksgiving let your requests be made known to God. And the peace of God, which surpasses all comprehension, will guard your hearts and your minds in Christ Jesus.

PHILIPPIANS 4:6-7

In some circumstances it is very easy to be anxious. You can take every situation that concerns you to Jesus. He will hear your prayers. He can flood your heart and mind with his peace, quiet your soul and provide you with rest.

...cast all your anxiety on Him, because He cares for you.

1 Peter 5:7

God is able to take all our worries and burdens upon himself. He cares for you so much. He is actively working in your life.

"Come to Me, all who are weary and heavy-laden, and I will give you rest. Take My yoke upon you and learn from Me, for I am gentle and humble in heart, and you will find rest for your souls. For My yoke is easy and My burden is light."

MATTHEW 11:28-30

Jesus says he will give rest to those who commit their lives to him. If you submit to Jesus, he will gently lead you to places of rest for your soul and mind.

These things I have spoken to you, so that in Me you may have peace. In the world you have tribulation, but take courage; I have overcome the world."
JOHN 16:33

Jesus tells us that even in trials, he can provide us with peace and courage. Jesus has overcome death and evil by dying on the cross and rising again. Because of this victory, we can have the ultimate peace, rest, and comfort for our soul.

Praying for you that...

~God will fill your heart with his peace, comfort and love.

~You will know that God is watching over you.

~God will show you that you can call out to him in any situation and that you can share all your worries with him.

~You can rest knowing that God is going to take care of you and guide you on the right path, if you commit your life to him.

Prince of Peace Control My Will

Prince of peace, control my will,
Bid the struggling heart be still;
Bid my fears and doubtings cease,
Hush my spirit into peace.
Thou hast bought me with Thy blood,
Opened wide the gate to God;
Peace I ask- but peace must be,
Lord, in being one with Thee.
May Thy will, not mine, be done,
May Thy will and mine be one;
Chase these doubtings from my heart,
Now Thy perfect peace impart.
Savior, at Thy feet I fall,
Thou my life, my God, my all!
Let Thy happy servant be
One forevermore with Thee!

MARY A. S. BARBER, 1839

Next Steps...

1) Find a Bible and start reading.

The New Testament in the Bible is a great place to start. The book of John gives a good introduction to Christianity. Also, the book of Psalm is another great read.

Access a free online Bible: www.biblestudytools.com. Look at the NIV or check out the New Living Translation. These are easier to understand.

2) Join a healthy church.

A healthy church teaches directly from the Bible and does not teach that you need to earn salvation. A healthy church is not controlling or "cult like".

A place to look for a church near you:

churches.goingfarther.net   or   www.calvarychapel.com

3) Join a Bible study to learn more about God.

There are some great and safe places for you to learn more about what the Bible says and to also have the opportunity to meet other Christians.

Alpha: www.alphausa.org/about   Campus Crusade: cru.org

Bible Study Fellowship: bsfinternational.org

The Lord bless you and keep you;
The Lord make His face shine on you,
and be gracious to you;
The Lord lift up His countenance on you,
And give you peace.

Numbers 6:24-26

In Dark Uncertainty, Know the Light of the World: 13 Days of Biblical Truths of the Christian Faith

Scripture quotations taken from the New American Standard Bible® (NASB), Copyright © 1960, 1962, 1963, 1968, 1971, 1972, 1973, 1975, 1977, 1995 by The Lockman Foundation
Used by permission. www.Lockman.org

Dictionary quotations taken from: Webster, Noah. An American Dictionary of the English Language: Intended to Exhibit, I. The Origin, Affinities and Primary Signification of English Words, As Far As They Have Been Ascertained; II. the Genuine Orthography and Pronunciation of Words, According to General. S. Converse, Printed by Hezekiah Howe, 1828.
Copyright: Public Domain
All Hymns Copyright: Public Domain

Questions? Comments? Please write to: knowJesushavehope@protonmail.com

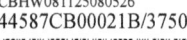

www.ingramcontent.com/pod-product-compliance
Lightning Source LLC
Chambersburg PA
CBHW081125080526
44587CB00021B/3750